EXPIATIONS

RAJANI KANTH

AUGUR PRESS

EXPIATIONS

Copyright © Rajani Kanth 2017

The moral right of the author has been asserted

All rights reserved
No part of this book may be reproduced in any form by photocopying or by any electronic or mechanical means, including information storage or retrieval systems, without permission in writing from both the copyright owner and the publisher of this book.

British Library Cataloguing in Publication Data.
A catalogue record for this book is available from the British Library.

ISBN 978-1-911229-00-1

First published 2017 by
Augur Press
Delf House
52 Penicuik Road
Roslin
Midlothian EH25 9LH
United Kingdom

Printed by Lightning Source

EXPIATIONS

To my many Muses:

My mother – Kannepalli Kesari

And my daughters – Antara, Indrina, Malini and Anjana

Contents

The Key

Foreword by Professor John McMurtry

Preface by the author

Myths

Millennium	1
The Lost	6
A Lament	7
Laws of Karma	11
Elegy for a Himalayan Childhood	13
Indian Summer	16
Flying	17
Exile	19
S/he	19
Time Travel	20
Being	22
Finale	24
Dolor	26
Yearning	27
Summer	28
Father	29
Frania	31
Divine Treasons	32
A Farewell	35

The Key

They first craft the Locks
Then fight over the Key –
That's the dreary story of –
All Philosophy

The Infinite is an Open
Door
In all simplicity –
the Mind may make what
locks it may
the Heart has the master
key

Foreword

I have been receiving Rajani Kanth's continuous poems over years and always read them despite demanding commitments. Their non-stop surprises of meter, rhyme and meaning, seer confidence of voice and expression, and music of pessimism and normally censored insight carry the reader in an outpouring of muse that is unique since William Blake. Verses stream forth in an incandescent but highly literate dark music of revelation as if moved from within by a direct witness not seen.

Although a well recognized professor of 'the dismal science' at Harvard, Rajani Kanth's poetry abandons the fortress of Western reason to let this inner voice flow, and flow it does in enthralling rage, compassion, distress and startling imagery borne in a lush, melodic poesy without peer. Steeped in memories brought to presence, Rajani's verse is trance-like in its songs of empire, family and expiation, primordially irrepressible in mood and dazzling in diction as one.

Verse and polemic stream forth together in breathtaking virtuosity of the English language whose depths few dare to imagine – a dark melancholy and doom of humanity crucified within the grinding chains and lies of normality and European civilization. But still shards of salvation peak trepid of the divine light of 'the One without a second', nurturing Woman and Tribal Love beneath division.

Driven by a full feeling of historical suffering from the inside, Rajani carries a burning bow to pierce the heartless vast machine of the modern Fall he sees all around him. He knows to the marrow the suffocating categories and vile hypocrisy of a miserly modernity ever mawing to more blood and oppression. Rajani speaks the heart of the living in a vigil of lone despair buoying up in preternatural song.

One feels a power of nature here, compelled to sing the end-time inside the global role machine where all strive to twist-fit into its forms omnivorously alienating the life Creation. He feels the tightening down breath of the world bursting the heart of the East-West witness he bears in torrents of poetry that seem to come from the other side of now.

John McMurtry is a Fellow of the Royal Society of Canada and author of The Cancer Stage of Capitalism/ from Crisis To Cure (London) and of Philosophy and World Problems, UNESCO Encyclopedia of Life Support Systems (Paris-Oxford).

Preface

This is but a sampler, and a rich smattering of verse – of all cadences and genres, penned over a long period of time.

These poems could, at best, howsoever fleetingly, warm the heart, soothe the disgruntled sensibility, or allay the anxieties of the disturbed mind.

The only interlarding thread, in all of them, is that rarefied sense of beauty that informs all poetic imagination.

The reader could pause on the sounds, the moods, or the meanings of the Lyrics: it doesn't matter – each is part of the mythopoetic resonance of the stanzas.

Occasionally, the Verses, old and new, are endorsed to near and dear ones, past and present: for such is the ever ongoing romance of life.

I will hope they stir the waking spirit in the reader: and compel him or her to Look around, yet again, at the mystery and splendour of our existence in this grandiloquent Planetary Endowment within which we occupy a tiny space as restless, reverberating nuclei of Pain and Desire that are our inexorable, conjoint Destiny as humans.

The selection is made across a very long canvas, dating back to 1968. Each is representative, as a loyal echo, of the period, the mood, and the context.

The verse is mere spoken music, as I think but in measures of metre and rhyme.

And words are deployed only as tonal instruments rather than items of syntax loaded with semantics.

So the reader may read, and *read in to,* as S/he pleases.

If these verses live on, it is my hope that the individuals they are dedicated to, shall also abide – forever.

Finally, the poetry of the universe is flung all around us: as Wordsworth had it: *'O Listen, for the vale profound is overflowing with the sound.'*

RK

Myths

They talk arrant, blithe,
Of Lives Fulfilled
I, merry, mordant
Laugh –
Say I
Have you, perchance
Seen a Cenotaph?
For such is Life
A Living Shroud for
The After-Life –
Only Death is fulsome
Full, Fulfilled
If it be not Written –
It is so Willed

Millennium

There they came, wave upon wave,
Titans of the mighty Tribe, goose-stepping
Cadres of Civilisation Mongers
flying flags, bearing bright Charters
vivid visions of scopious Human Redemption
peremptory in short command
Organised like generals
with no intelligence overlooked
to press all Rhetoric into instant Service
of the Great Emancipatory Cause
of Liberty, Life and Lust for Unilateral Happiness

We, the Little People, mired in Microcosms
watched, waved, jumped and clapped
as they marched in Grand Parade
down from our meagre perches
in the craven cul-de-sacs of jaded
loss of hope, reason and
ordinary norms of Co-respecting
Decency, with our own Philosophy
of Bread, and the sweet Elixir
of Collective Amnesia
as they rocketed on overhead

Ribbons and flags, curled and fluttered,
lay festooning the grandiloquent
boulevards of Wealth and State
as we scampered like mice
After the March, to nibble the Souvenirs
of the Great Epoch just unveiled
by the Orchestra of Imperial Design –
Here Democracy, there Liberty
Property, Rule of Law, all gaudy and glistering –
and how we rushed to collect the swag
run home, and gorge like expectant Children

We celebrated in swoon all night long
this Arrival of the Promised Day
raising cheap, copious, libations to the health
of our Great Captains who smiled rich, ravishing smiles
and bared immaculately polished teeth of steel
shimmering, glaring television screens distending
the raucous audio of their Manifest Assembly
in deafening bytes of syncopating
timbre, tone, and Declamatory Excess

Then the last tanks rolled, clunking away –
the P.A. systems fell sudden silent
and the grim Mondays of sombre Sobriety
returned to haunt the ineffable Drudgery
of our new Speedocratic workaday week –
The Great Machine cranked, creaked
its stilted wheels back on rails again
as we sang the Song of the Shirt
quiet now under our unsweetened breath

And then came the clumping, clustering Pictures
blinking like sorties of streaming glow-worms
dotting in digitals our Great Advantage
bright proclaimed over the Perilous Planet
as we set down dinner forks to
digest its meaning for our limping lives
as laser rockets razed the riveting screen
and great plumes of Distal Destruction
filled adult minds with unthinkable dread
as children huddled struck dumb seeking
comfort in their parents' flinching eyes

Like merrymakers tossed dizzy off whirling roundabouts
we re-inform our distrusting hearts of Logic, and the
Great Game of Reason, played by the aerial Mandarins of State
seeking shreds, shrapnels, shards of meaning
in the obscure behemoths of hopeless Corruption
of Speech, Image, Word, and new-fangled Archetype –
but infertile assurance born of Impotence breeds not
the sterile contentments of yore: and we stoop warily
to wonder how and why and when we lost
even the merest semblance of control

The music eternal blares and streaking strobes
scan the hypertrophic universe, lit up like holograms
of this barren Realm of Discontent,
born of seething Madness, the Toxic nostrums of Smith, Locke
the Buonopartism of Commerce and the Calvanism
of rampant Greed become now the fodder Popcorn and Soda
of our daily viewing – like incapacitated Voyeurs
nailed to our seats, staring fixedly ahead
at the desolation of our own Disempowering lives

How now to move to Love or Care?
Billows of cleaving empathy made alien by the
Hobbesian pall envelope us like a miasma,
Seeding descending clouds of disabling distrust –
Crucified in desiccating Hate, we dry up
in near and far domains, shedding sanguine lives
of Vitals that fire the fusions of stirred Emotion
stoking the furnace of warmth, affection and passion –
We live but in wan Dress Rehearsal of Death

The Guardians prattle on in their glib Discourse
of Death: enchain resolve, entombing
the native springs of Sovereign Actions
denude, intoxify Earth, Sea, and Sky
dismembering our Collective Memory
of Mutual Convenance in trade for
crass, consumptive stupefactions: now bought
now sold for spoonfuls of lusting, desire
and sprigfuls of All-requiting Bigotry

Slim pontoons of slender Hope still straddle
the yawning Abyss of Despair; as they run their Last Race
upon our Free-gifted Spaces, we gather up the fringes
in rousing Counter-Prophecy: Nothing lives or dies in vain –
the Clockwork Universe of Order and Exactitude
Self-Aware, corrects all ravages in Rectifying Time;
and we as Conscious Atoms may yet breathe into that
Incorrigible Cosmic Plan our Ragged Philanthropy
of Indemnifying Love in lucent, lustrating streams of
unstinting, Immaculate, Beatitude

The Lost

The Zoe
of
the Amazon

Are not
Adorned
As We

A mile from
Home, they
Weep and wail

Pray, how Far
gone
Are We?

A Lament

Like the atom
We are hollow,
then:
but Holograms of
Hollow men

so very fit
To enter it
there be none
to mentor it
The molten pit
Of hu-Man Wit

Inexorable suicide:
In convenances
dare defied
contraventions
justified –
Yet myths of progress
Still abide:
Debaucheries,
but bona fide

No saviour
Can now arise
No blood to shed
That purifies
no cross that yet
indemnifies
as turpitude
just multiplies

as seas boil
forests burn
there can be
no just return
our time is gone
and grimly past
the deadly
die is dearly
cast

all is now
forever lost
to extinction
and holocaust
Rubicons
long criss-crossed:
fearful blunders,
frightful cost

things built,
rudely broken:
old blasphemies
rewoken
earth but
a sallow
token
our doom
itself
bespoken

in lament,
departing:
bid bedlamites
goodbye
they that made
this goodly world
a foetid, putrid
sty

but know just who
they be
and what they
daily do
for whom
Helvete
is Valhalla:
elixir,
the devil's brew

Ahabs steer
The ship of state
In lottery
Of human fate
Hubris fills
Voids
in men,
who, venturing,
capitulate:
as reason wakes,
in fits and shakes
far, far too late

'twere time enow
to bid adieu
the devil without
will have
his due:
theirs it is,
to be Evil:
ours, to be
but True

in love, let us
then mutiny
in joy, resist
the mire:
in peace, war
with destiny:
in defeat,
embrace desire

Laws of Karma

Tomorrow's Sun
Will surely rise
No Epiphany
No Surprise
Ancient Evil's
New Reprise
All Swept Away
in a Passing
Breeze
It's Over Now
The Games
are Done
Matters not
who Lost
or Won
Earth Commences
All Anew
The Planet but
Awaits the Cue
It comes not Slow
It comes not Fast
It cometh but to
Erase the Past
The Age Renews
An Ancient Pledge
Splayed with Ruth
On a Razor's Edge

And All shall be Held
Yea, All shall be Bound
To Great Laws of Sky
as We run Aground
And into Pathways Lost
And Gateways Found
We shall Meander,
Delirious, Unbound

Elegy for a Himalayan Childhood

The halls of yesteryear
In the Himalayan heights.
Stand hushed, deserted:
And we who gambolled
In their humble, hallowed Ways,
Once upon a time, light in heart and mind
Felt them full, and plim: with furtive lights,
Night charades, and pillow fights,
Unremembered wrongs, unminding slights,
Gay caparisoned, trite, short, and sweet,
with memories of changeling, childhood days
battening cloudbursts of madcap triumph,
Mock derisions, reverberating laughter,
In a coronal, blessed, haze,
where what comes, rarely ever stays,
not caring what came before, or after:

Life laughed not with us, but at us,
from above, where dour eagles gaze
With pitiless eye: but free yet of pain,
we paid no heed: indeed was there no need,
To think about then, or hereafter:
The pie was in the sky, there could be no
desiring: fun to romp, to roll, to rush,
and headlong fall into the cradling haze
of the green earth: where could never
be hint of darkness, or disabling dearth.

Now locked within fretful memory's Eye,
I ask: what if we had known the coming stealth
Of crushing fate, before it became too late:
what might we have, all wan, dismantled then,
To know we live but in a World of Men? –
where the few disdain the many,
to stand aghast one day, alone, sans comfort
Cold or warm, stricken by malintentioned, wilful harm?
As days turn, weeks to months, to long years,
of bittering servitude, in the teeming urban glen
of daily darkness: who did build this
vast, grey, dour, bastille of our longest days?
Joy fleeteth, ever now, by the Unmarked hour
And we struggle but to Brave and Breathe
The Chill air of all-stultifying Dejections,
for the sad remainder of our feckless days?

How are we, yearly, daily, betrayed,
sans succour, sans any hope of mortal aid
struck down by lies of truant society,
cheating hearts, and malignant state?
And yet are we crucified, without benediction,
No space betwixt the fact, the fiction,
To fall into those designed hells of
coruscating despair, where, all debauched,
we huddle, sullen, and stare, in mind vacuous, spirit bare
In bright sunlight, and god's own free, unfettering, air –

Take me now to my stupefactions of insouciance
Before these expiating memories fade
Where the gaunt idylls of life were all mislaid
Where errant joys were but ever careless played
Where pipe dreams were daily made, unmade
Where the glad heart a fulsome dower paid
To trust, care, salves of primeval sympathy,
One to one, one to the other, fond sister to doting brother,
under a clear, and guileless sky, as benighted children,
blissfully ensconced in a propitiating bower,
who simply, sweetly, unstintingly – yes:
loved one another

Indian Summer

for Indrina

There are shades so soft you may not see
once the lustrous day is spent
and the pinkly blush along the sky
is passed away to sorrower things –
clutch then the heavy heart of earth
and feel anew its throbbing beat
there are sounds so slight you may not hear
but raise the dust and stir the wind
that veils the calm of hush and still
yet in that haze, the mystery
and in that breath, the clue –
there is script so strange you may not read
though long you gaze with vacant eye
before the glazing dust is in
and the stars deflect the protean mood
and the moon effects a change in scene –
there are smiles so sad you may not feel
the mask with which true love is hid
but let these go, the hour is come
to sip and taste the stagnant air
and drink the scent of mango leaves

Flying

for Malini

Love hangs
like a gossamer
from a rainbow
in the sky –
if only
words
could fly!

Sunsets reek
of butterflies
amber
leaves look
like wings
and I think
somewhere
in the park
a nightingale
sings

The day is
spread
like honey
now leaking
from a jar
emphatically sunny
and things
are up to
par

I cannot see
your love
light
and barely
feel
the pain –
perhaps this
summer madness
will not
come back
again

Love hangs
like a gossamer
it's my
rainbow
in the sky
scattering my
kisses
like petalled
wings that
fly

Exile

for Antara

I'm like a snared Cassowary
Flightless in Bantustan –
It would take a Missionary
To reconcile me to Man

Sightless is the Visionary
Banished from her Clan
Lightless, the Seminary
which falters in its Plan

Like a failed Apothecary
Whose panaceas do not pan
I ache for that sanctuary –
where Eve both delved and span

S/he

for Anjana

She, that rocks the cradle
cares Not to rule the World –
for Her, Love Suffices,
no requital, nor gold:
'Tis He that chafes to Rule,
A once ardent heart on hold:
shorn, with no binding tie
(tears leeched to an inner eye),
ventures blind, in the cold:
where Instinct is Destiny,
What Reason breaks the mould?

Time Travel

This mind
is a motel
and stray thoughts
like night lodgers
(artful dodgers)
linger a while

Come morning
the bills are paid
(and beds are made)
and only
the desolate
are found delayed

The some that
stay
like aging tenants
sleep the day
doze until
the fire abates
nor heed the
tooting
at the morning gates

But come and go
they must, and
do
now lost, now found
but travellers true

And travel
they must –
only this motel master
gathers dust:
like a picture
from a fallen frame
through which
all that passes
stays the same

Being

[*Exordium*]
Doctors Faustus
have gone and
Lost us:
Made Strangeloves
Of us all…

[*Aria*]
Inch by inch
We dissipate
Hour to hour,
we wake too late

Frame by frame
We fuse in hate
and though, by will:
still think it fate

so, taken are we
one by one
as we cower,
cringe,
and wait

to bell-jars
in an iron cage
with dystrophy
as bait –

death is all the
respite here –
that nought else
can abate

whence in plots
perennial
citing
'reasons of state'

the barbarians
turn away,
perforce,
the civilised
at the gate

whence is virtue
banished by
the vampires
at the gate –
as just desserts,
unholy strewn,
rot with manna –
on heaven's plate

we can neither
rise to reason
nor fall to the
floor in faith
in such a stinting
season, in lowly,
dark, estate –
in treachery and
in treason
can we only –
Capitulate

Finale

They came for him after dark, 'twas a blustery day
the rafters were not done shaking and rain beat against
the little panes in all turbid force as if to wake, warn
the listener within to alarm and instant flight –
the old tree shook its spindry branches over the roof
thumping full sore, and the little wicket gate swung wide
on its rusty hinges creaking with all its wooden might

He had spent an ordinary day really no less no more
little silly things that men do when left alone in eventide
with enough of this and not enough of that,
part habit part whimsy part just uninspiring madness
he had to keep thinking little things lest the world
noticed that he really had not much left to think or do
that he had not done already, to stave the all-engulfing void

The prosaic, become the hum-drum bane of his isolate way,
did little to hype the life-force or help him fight the
overweening fever and fatigue risen like a foetid stench
and steeped right into the nourished grain of his white and
wooden walls, which nursed his soundless cries for years
reflecting back cheerless light, as he lay stifled, stiff, and still
against them: they, unmoved by the daily, torpid, rise and fall

The breaking seasons affected little the tenor of that tepid life
save that heat and cold kept their strict apportioned bay
as he bent and bowed through ablutions of exacting night
and depleting day, in repetition, rot, and slow decay
dreams moving like clouds gliding the restive mind
from high to low and low to high again in unstinting motion
as if the race were not done and games still left to play

Children and barking dogs ran aground without
in heady search of sport as he heedless unsmiling
sat staring at musty portraits hanging still
of young, old, near and far, unable to read the frozen faces,
nor could see: but that the fading mind's failing eye
had sovereignty over vision, memory and breaking thoughts,
fallen to harsh arbiters the eliding ellipse of reason,
remembrance and rue, which neither truly seeks nor finds

The good neighbours from behind bland, blockading screens
of decorum, doubt, and distrust, wondered the why and what
of that wispy warp of wanting, wasting, life,
shuddering at what they guessed lay behind
the little house with the close shuttered windows
whispering to wide-eyed children not to stray after dusk
for you never could tell, really, for these are the bad old days
where heaven knows, there is no one left to trust

And so they came that wet and wintry night
and whisked him clean away: not a blind opened
nor a door held one whit ajar to watch him
leave: he barely knew it himself were the wind not so strong,
and the rain not beat so hard upon his wan and wondering face
but the house stood deathly still and the whitewashed walls
hugged their pastel secrets, the portraits looked to one another,
but held their painted peace and the spinning wheels,
surged over with conspiring silence, sped swiftly away

Dolor

I too have dwelt in Arcady
'twas but a vagrancy of mind
Adrift in parched, algid space
Nor cohort close behind

Iron distemp'ring fractured steel
Ingresses the sojourning soul
what yearning heart can, quenched, beat,
rude rent, racked, Unwhole?

There's alchemy that muteth guilt
Conjury that absterseth pain
But where the cloying anodyne
Quells rue's self-contusing train?

Lifeblood beads up like burgundy
Eructing gore from the gashed vein
Grievous gutted, love's ardency
Exsiccates, its hallowed drain

I too have dwelt in Arcady
In phantasms of the doting mind
immured in its artless travesty
in the glut of my decline

Yearning

A hunger burst upon me wild
the source I could not descry
I rose from a sleepless slumber
to ask the wherefore and why

I had stood my life at windows
not ever daring to eat
but staring at such diners
Deep delved in wine and meat

This fruit of the bread that breaks
I saw it healed them not
the juice of the grape that slakes
I saw it steeled them not

I had put aside in the past
the grosser appetite
for the soul had so dearly wished
to be but laden light

But give me now your breadstick
your chalice of chafing wine
tonight I think it's high time
to welter with the swine

Summer

It is summer –
yet ill blows the
forest blaze
of truant colour:
marigolds wave
embalmed
orchard heads
dowager queens
frittering grace
upon richer laity
frolicked
in nectaring
meadows:
nature struts,
high prodigal:
but, the narrow,
homespun heart
stays stilted,
undrenched –
in wake of
the one bloom
that makes chill winter
of the splendoured hour:
tears find no requital,
even in opulence
of light –
and I but famish:
at the feast

Father

For fearless
my father lay
on that dark
and devilish day
when death
a demon from the
deep
broke behind
his silent sleep

He froze before
the dusk befell
and all those
haunting ghosts
from hell
withdrew for
once
their awful spell

And so that
span of
flesh and bone
heart and wholeness
died alone
as pride with
passion
turned to stone

No cannon spoke
no curlew call
rose to sound
my father's fall
as if the frame
whose bolts I bear
just burned to
ash
all unaware

I wept not then
and tears unshed
stilled the tale
with words unsaid
as love and life
and laughter
lost
to pain and pride
and passions past

But, in these
blessed beads
of rhyme
I freeze the flow
of father time
his voice
within
their circle
caught
nor remembered
nor forgot

Frania

An old woman
in a cold room
talking of the
president
and what her
shrinking
life has meant
slipping through
the shreds
of her soft and spindry
words
torn from
that hideous
working wheel
whereunder
hoarse and hungry
hours
she spent
twisting through
a hundred years
of fear
and childspun
fantasy

Divine Treasons

Forsworn to me
the ways of men
forfeit, sanctuaries
of mind:

So dwelt I ever in
Arcady
Amongst the Host
Divine:

They rein me back
idylls of yore
From sloughs
of deep despond:

but still I fain
adventure there
for the heart –
it be too fond

Perhaps on some
St Agnes' eve
love may find its
Truant way

Though the wolf
waits by the vestibule
and hounds do howl
and bay

the night is dark
the knell sounds low
Nemesis seeks
Its chosen prey

The moon is hid
In darkling cloud
The moors glow
Sombre grey

There's a tide in the
lambent stream of life
slim reeds of hope
abound

but unannounced
in the surge of weal
the water wraiths
confound

perhaps the night
might yet reveal
why I keep
eternal wake?

Lo, the stars depart,
the heavens part:
and I am riven –
At the stake

been the way
With gods and men
Since time itself
Began

human hearts
all, helpless, grieve:
as the gods,
smiling: Deceive

A Farewell

We will Heed no more the Call of the Wild
to fulsome seductions in Whimsey's wan pall
few Artless amongst us yet Lost in the Woods,
in goblin ensnarings, rapt by Sirens in Thrall –

We stride swiftly by Quicksands, past Pythons of Blight,
abeying the Tempters in Revels of Night:
The Long Dance quite ended, the Tables full Bare,
The Candles still flicker, but the Music is spare –

Carriage wheels clatter, gates creak to let go,
Wry catcalls ricocheting, Wraiths take to the Tow:
lolled in their penumbra, we grew sere in its glow,
but the Dread Lot is past, new Salves are aflow:

Time pratfalls in Trespass, life still is Unclear,
But the Vigil is demitting, neap Redemptions appear:
We fain sense the sunrise, we feel it loom nigh:
Burnishing the damson of a still smould'ring sky:

The Masque is untwining, the Ghouls are in flight,
Vampire and Werewolf, all glid into Night:
We who Adored them now resolve to Revile –
For We shall Yield no more to the Call of the Wild

www.ingramcontent.com/pod-product-compliance
Lightning Source LLC
Chambersburg PA
CBHW031506040426
42444CB00007B/1231